A Sanctuary Green
595 contemporary haiku

A Sanctuary Green
595 contemporary haiku

Ed Bremson

iUniverse, Inc.
New York   Bloomington

iUniverse books may be ordered through booksellers or by contacting:

iUniverse
1663 Liberty Drive
Bloomington, IN 47403
www.iuniverse.com
1-800-Authors (1-800-288-4677)

Because of the dynamic nature of the Internet, any Web addresses or links contained in this book may have changed since publication and may no longer be valid. The views expressed in this work are solely those of the author and do not necessarily reflect the views of the publisher, and the publisher hereby disclaims any responsibility for them.

ISBN: 978-1-4401-6943-4 (sc)
ISBN: 978-1-4401-6944-1 (ebook)

Printed in the United States of America

iUniverse rev. date: 09/14/09

For Cedric,
2009 –

thank you for being
a good, generous friend
almost thirty years

I

amber light
leaves to rake
far away a train

winter rain, summer sun
birds perched high on wires
looking down on us

blackbird in the street
pecking at rotten carcass
startled, it takes flight

piles of leaves
a boy jumps in
laughing

a child
sees a pile of leaves
and smiles

cool November night
walking in the neighborhood
dog shit on my shoe

cricket in the house —
is it still lucky
even if I kill it?

driving into night
leaden eyes startle open
god I need coffee

in the cotton field
she steals one sprig of cotton
runs back laughing

November sky
just before sunset
full moon

midnight sounds —
boat on a lake, flashlight click,
frog being gigged

next year, when autumn comes
and leaves cover my yard
I will be gone

a passing neighbor
takes one look at all my leaves
and says, "wow!"

rain drips in the drain
and in the yard
a sparrow sings

raking leaves to the street –
watching the wind blow them
back into the yard

raking leaves
a gift of one more year
the smell of earth

near my bed
a scratching in the night
I'll sleep on the couch

standing in leaves
up to my knees –
nearby a whirlwind dies

while raking the yard —
the smell of pine straw
and fresh dirt

at the funeral home
my wife in the casket —
oh, who combed her hair?

power line —
one bird lands
in his own spot

large house
but for mice
there is no room

clearing brush
in the back yard
one eye looks for snakes

a dead vine
still tries to cling
if it gets a chance

piles of leaves
after the rain
too heavy to rake

countless autumn buds
on a large camellia bush
with one white blossom

dry, flat bird carcass
lying on the sidewalk
outside of Whole Foods

the tree gives me leaves
I rake them
we're both happy

winter sky –
two birds chasing one bird
and their cries . . .

don't let anyone
or anything
ruin your life

hauling leaves
from the back yard to the front
me and my neighbor

geese honking
flying past
at sunset

old man gives thanks
he has lived long enough
to learn some simple things

on the highway
a mangled deer carcass
drivers whizzing by

indian summer day –
still in parking lot tree
a blackbird

grocery store broccoli bin –
one red ladybug
and another one!

indian summer day –
a dearth of raindrops
but not of falling leaves

a dog
walking down the street alone
dragging its own leash

half moon
so pale
midday winter sky

homeless beggar
buying three large cans of
Colt 45

Sunday evening
dancing in the kitchen
with Ludwig van

old man
driving at night
gazing at the stars

gray winter day
so mournful
distant train whistle

cold winter sky
so light tonight
blanket of clouds

it rained all day
now the sky has cleared –
full moon tonight

doves taking flight
sounding as only doves sound –
Christmas day

clouds
charcoal smudges gray against
evening winter sky

daffodils
blooming in January
so cool

how light the sky is
cloudless winter night
missing stars

lying on the floor
of the grocery store
some kind of small bone

afternoon sky
through bare winter branches
the moon

blackbirds
strutting around my yard
like they own the place

on Shelley Lake
so many gulls
so far from the sea

I saw a blue bird
(not a blue jay)
and I was happy

bright blue sky
one gull chases one gull
mercilessly

on the street –
pulpy picked over squirrel
and blackbirds

old man's yard –
all the grass has died
but the weeds survived

alone
in the middle of a field
one blackbird

they sowed grass seed
and reaped
yard full of black birds

winter sky
raining and raining
after Ginger died

new moon —
old friend buried
this afternoon

outside in the rain
a black guy barfing
beer and pizza

god-damned blackbird
in the middle of the street
even in the rain

reckless driver
kind enough to hit a tree
not a person

in the woods
a path down among the leaves
empty beer cans

in the yard
a large dead rabbit —
keep the kids away

geese
beautiful swimmers
horrific roadkill

at Shelley Lake
all the gulls are gone –
first day of spring

honey moon
disappears behind a cloud
too soon

on the highway
some small creature
red-splattered

cool of the evening
birds flying tree to tree
singing songs of spring

down the street
a tree covered with blossoms
red and pink

in the cherry tree –
a blackbird lands
among pink blossoms

many flowers
at the arboretum
blackbirds

homeless man
in the woods
sitting on a stump

butterfly
flutters by
too fast

the cool air tonight
reminding me of spring
forty years ago

how ugly
the crape myrtle is
in the wintertime

a hawk flies away
against the evening sky
with contrails

a bubbling spring
once deep in the woods
when I was a boy

silly geese
walk across dangerous streets
when they could fly

dead goose in the street
feathers ruffled by the breeze
from passing cars

flock of geese
walking across the street –
rush hour traffic

nighttime on my porch –
fireflies
and a full moon

after the storm
evening fireflies rise
from the wet grass

nightfall –
the birds stop singing
and the crickets start

neighborhood air
full of wildfire smoke
and birdsong

a sanctuary green
cool
water trickling over stones

II

two dandelions –
one ragged puffball
one yellow flower

dappled Crabtree Creek
carrying sunlight
downstream

rushing waters
very different than
rushing traffic

girl on a bicycle
near Crabtree Creek
the smell of her perfume

tall tree
its top catches
afternoon sunlight

on the far bank
hanging over the creek
Spanish moss

some commotion
way up there on a limb
a blackbird

near the trail
after the storm
sound of chainsaw

January
dandelion
yellow sunshine

on flowing water
sunlight dances
while birds sing

on the far bank
barking at me
poodles

today on the trail:
bicyclists, a dead muskrat,
loud girls, and stray dogs

a bloody blackbird wing
lies beside the trail –
a hawk cries overhead

in Rothgeb Park
February blooms
redbuds and daffodils

old stones large and small
beside the trail
glittering sunlight

rabbit tobacco
beside the trail
memories of my youth

in Crabtree Creek
one young duck alone
loudly quacking

blue sky, wispy clouds
in the air
a red bug hovers

a muskrat creeps
down the bank into the creek –
goes downstream sideways

in Mine Creek
clear water flows
over green stones

sound of beating wings
I turn and see
blackbird on a limb

blue tailed lizard
on the trail
zigs and zags away

spring wildflowers
in Rothgeb Park
a bumblebee

flying high
blackbird
shadow on the trail

two geese eating straw
and defecating
on the trail

giants
in our midst
dropping leaves on our heads

winter still
in Mine Creek
two mallards swimming

in Crabtree Creek
lined up on one log
six geese

raindrops
on the trail
white flower petals

from a lofty pine branch
two blackbirds defecate
in white profusion

five dandelions
dropped on the trail
left to wilt in the sun

on a rock in the sun
a large turtle
and her little one

in Crabtree Creek
two turtles on a rock
and a football floating

blackbird silence
gliding from tree to tree
sound of feet landing

small bird
chases large bird
out of sight

redbud trees
on the trail
bicycle bells

two ducks, two geese
on Mine Creek
shadow of a hawk

odors of flowers
and girls
running on the trail

redbuds
and red bugs
oh, the southern life

turtles, geese, Spanish moss –
how low
the creek is today

babbling creek water
before my eyes
swarm of tiny bugs

blooming dogwoods
in my back yard
barking dogs

windy yesterday
rained all day today
pollen everywhere

stiff breeze blowing
puffball
hanging on

those kids on the trail
they can't kill all the puffballs
or can they?

in Rothgeb Park
a white azalea bush
with one pink blossom

sound of blackbird
I turn and see
blooming redbud tree

beside the trail
two wood-handled shovels
both soaked from the rain

raindrops
on the trail
redbud petals

brown toadstools
beside the trail
a light mist

monarch butterfly
flying over Crabtree Creek
lucky devil

on a brown toadstool
my first dragonfly
of the year

in thirty years
Rothgeb Park has changed a lot –
but then so have I

blue jays and red birds
on Mine Creek
glittering sunlight

turtle in Mine Creek
crawling under water
sunlight and shadow

a hawk flies
from tree to tree
shadowed by a crow

out for a walk
ladybug
crawling on the trail

on the trail
a pit bull
on a leash, thank god

a hawk perched so high
so unruffled
by blackbirds

ducks and geese
swimming in the creek
a muskrat

ivy
clinging to a pine
a dragonfly

this stream
usually so quiet
loud after the rain

mockingbird
alone on a fence
singing and singing

field of white flowers
in Rothgeb Park
one white butterfly

trees overhead
green inchworms falling
on my neck

where Mine Creek
enters into Crabtree Creek
a snake swimming

waiting all year
for the sweet black plums of June
that may or may not come

after the storm
evening clouds part
there's Jupiter

after the storm
my street covered
with pinecones

last day of June
crape myrtles blooming
beside the highway

after the rain
drops of water
falling from the trees

big black man
driving long brown Cadillac
with a white roof

a blackbird
standing on the grass
in front of the church

one good thing –
when cyclists suddenly pass
they're quickly gone

for safety's sake
watch out for snakes
when you leave the trail

a cool afternoon
with lots of sunshine on rocks –
a prime time for snakes

a patch of snow
deep in the woods
birdsong

first warm day in weeks
multitude of birds
feasting in the grass

breezy afternoon
over my neighborhood
a blackbird soaring

my back yard
a black cat stalks a mouse
in the snow

walking on the trail
two little red bugs
connected butt to butt

yellow jackets crawl
on yellow dandelions
first day of spring

shadow on the trail
much larger than
the bird in the sky

on my TV screen
Ginger Rogers still dances
like a dream

breezy afternoon
parking lot covered
with cherry blossoms

magenta petals
carpeting the ground
beneath a redbud tree

lovely blue sky
such a hot spring day
thank god for some shade

morning floodwaters
cowboys herding cattle
using jet skis

Sunday in the park –
a pregnant woman
looking so hot

old man
standing in his yard
watching young men work

taking out the trash
odor of cigarette smoke
the flowers next door

spider on the floor –
I killed it
but it wasn't easy

gray clouds in a blue sky
cool breeze
inchworms dropping from trees

a white butterfly
following me
beneath white dogwood trees

in the creek
a decoy duck floats
beneath hanging Spanish moss

cool cloudy day
dogwoods and azaleas bloom
all over town

breezy afternoon –
mowed grass smells good
mower fumes smell bad

after the storm
a large limb lying
broken on the street

on my backyard table
dancing
raindrops and sunshine

sleepless night –
some pictures worth
a thousand nightmares

above the trail
dancing together
three white butterflies

glancing at my wife
when he thinks I'm not looking –
one of the yard men

woodpecker
please leave my house alone
so I can sleep

as I drive on my street
a large blackbird swoops down
and crosses my path

pale moon
peeking out from behind clouds —
pale blue twilit sky

an ugly centipede
on my toilet paper roll —
omg!

storm debris
on the street
birds standing

Mother's day —
magnolias blossoming
smelling so sweet

frolicking
on the banks of Crabtree Creek
several monarchs

my solitude
disturbed today
by helicopters

thank you, little cat,
for coming to my yard
and eating my mice

coming down a limb
sideways
a blue jay

streetlight
reflected in a puddle
the moon

rainy Sunday
reading by the window
power outage

woman on the trail
talking on the phone
her dog running free

man on the trail
riding his bike
too fast

beagle on a leash
pulling left
pulling right

mmmm, honeysuckle –
glad
I took this trail today

big shadow
small bird
flying by

spring afternoon
ceiling fan turning
in an empty room

thank you, little birds
for eating the bugs
in my yard

street near the drugstore
littered
with rubber gloves

that light –
didn't it get brighter
before it failed?

afternoon sky
one little black cloud
among all the white ones

early June
nice cool breeze
like springtime

old man
grateful he feels really good
one more birthday

hooray!
the red birds are back!
all must be forgiven.

hot spring days
really a drag
but the nights are cool

toward sunset
out of a leafy green tree
black wings beating

two baby birds
landing in my back yard
poking in the grass

bold or crazy
cockroach
on my foot

lucky day
in my back yard
a dove

little black birds
pecking in the grass
in the rain

twilight
visiting again
the red bird

car 4 sale
with dogs
sticking out its windows

leaves shake suddenly
squirrel jumping
limb to limb

darkness
outside my window
a firefly passing

line of geese
walking up the street
in the wrong lane

outside the window
two robins
hopping by

birds eating berries
leave droppings on my car
as they fly away

two white noise machines
in the doctor's office
wtf??

bloody flesh
on the street
blackbirds gathering

lunchtime
a bowl of soup
a tick on my neck

III

in the winter time
with the leaves gone from the trees
how beautiful the sky

one bird
flying back and forth
building her nest

in Crabtree Creek
floating slowly downstream
cherry blossoms

in my back yard
blooming today
several dogwoods

on a late spring night
my household disturbed –
leaky plumbing

cool, sunny day
a butterfly passes me
as I walk

my life
feels like a twinkling star
is more like a shooting star

a bird squawking
in the neighborhood
after the hailstorm

Sunday afternoons
much better for me now
than when I was young

back yard
covered with wildflowers
old friends sit chatting

oh little squirrels
go away
please don't eat my house

red leaves on the ground
beneath a tree in my yard
after today's storm

the hail falls
as if to the bottom
of a storm-tossed sea

rising sun –
an old friend
I haven't seen in years

in this world
there's less dying
than being born

Shelley Lake
the sea gulls leave
when the leaves return

winter roses –
a dazzling sight
to anyone's eyes

on Christmas eve
drinking wine
apparently too much

impossible to keep
the leaves from the trees
when spring arrives

in the birdbath
new year's frozen water –
later, little bird

a new year begins
blooming soon
new flowers

my wife drowned herself
in the city's reservoir
nice thought, huh?

IV

this trail
so little traffic
winter afternoon

rainy evening
home alone with tears
chopping onions

cricket
in my hand
struggles to be free

spring moonlight –
a black cat waits silently
in the yard

spring twilight
butterfly
lights on a daffodil

my dead wife
in my thoughts
my loss and hers

spring sunshine
dreading
summer heat

spring thunderstorm
pelting the cherry trees
but we need the rain

foggy night
TV tower out of sight
airplane drone

it rained
just enough to make a mess
of all the pollen

it would flee
if I tried to grab it —
jumping cricket

winter —
bare trees standing
in afternoon fog

hardwood floors
no central air
my first taste of pizza

a lizard
sticks its nose out
into the sun

field of white flowers –
flying away
one white butterfly

waking in the dark
waiting
for the pain to subside

walking by the creek
one last time
before summer

neighborhood fragrance –
is that jasmine?
gardenia?

purple wildflower
trampled
but still lovely

April showers –
on the ground beneath the tree
fallen petals

driving all day
finding a hotel
and a glass of wine

seeing a blue heron
flying over Shelley Lake
never gets old

in the neighborhood
children's laughter
and birdsong

a homeless man
sitting on the curb
eating a salad

my house so nice
even the squirrels
want to live inside

wetness of the pinecones
lying in the yard
after the storm

moonlight so cool
on my lawn
casting shadows

on the trail
a tiny snake
flicking its tiny tongue

after the rain
sunlight shining
through a hole in the roof

plum trees –
I don't recognize them
but I love black plums

taking a nap
hearing the phone ring
in my pocket

first spring thunderstorm –
where did all the birds
and homeless people go?

morning sunlight
too bright
to gaze at the sky

quiet evening
young boy frightened by a tick
on his privates

not just her leaving
freight train
but your distant, mournful song

poignant memory?
so many spring nights –
which one to choose?

winter rain –
everything still so gray
but not for long

first snow
falling
but not sticking

spring solitude
watching all the colors
as they return

after the leaves are gone
there's still plenty to see
if you look

seafood store
parking lot
rotten fishy smell

those who love winter
spend a lot of time
gazing at the sky

it may be hot
but still I stop and gaze
at the blue cloudless sky

spring ending
so soon
April heat wave

town without trains –
how can it know joy
without sadness?

summer grass sprouting
so early this year
rainfall surplus

a mouse
scratching in the wall
near my bed

summer garden
watching fireflies
blinking in the dark

Crabtree Creek –
sometimes fast, sometimes slow
sometimes high, sometimes low

at the Marriott
sounds of love through the wall –
tossing and turning

cool autumn evening
warming the house
with cooking

butterflies
like most other flying things
but so quiet

spring regret –
we did not say goodbye
before she died

in spring
trees shed so many petals
it's like a mini fall

blackbird
has trouble landing –
windy day

cool again today
after several hot days
end of April

old man's morning pain –
sometimes goes away quick
sometimes lasts all day

a quiet morning
sipping green tea
watching red birds in the yard

two halves of a melon
sweet and refreshing
whichever one I choose

old man eats breakfast
blackberry seeds
hurt his teeth

garlic growing
in my kitchen
under the dishwasher

new year's eve —
do birds feel the cold
like I do?

birds, bugs, flowers, trees —
and in the grand scheme of things
where do I fit in?

the world
has always had its dangers
and always will

still light outside
but not for long —
leave the porch light on

in a tree near the trail
I heard a screech today —
still a mystery

childhood –
persimmon tree in my yard
but no persimmons

spring twilight –
why is that young girl running
down the street in her dress?

a field of cotton
white as if it had snowed
in September

early spring evening
my neighbors walk separately
I hope all is well . . .

sweet betsy blossoms –
remember the days
before everything changed?

V

gathering clouds –
the sound of thunder
after its long journey

white dogwood blossoms –
a girl beneath the street light
walking her dog

cherry blossoms –
are they white?
pink?

that wormlike creature,
mindless, writhing so,
only wants to live

tears
for the years, friends, and loved ones
forever gone

cloudy, sunny,
cloudy, sunny, in my yard
all morning

squirrels
bother me all day
and in my dreams

in my kitchen
a large spider –
why didn't it run away?

cloudy spring sky
threatening rain
all day

sawdust on the porch
and the lingering odor
of insect spray

the man next door
working on his car
with his dogs nearby

Sunday afternoon –
glad to be alone now
with so much time

I don't know the names
of many flowers
in my yard

sound of garbage trucks
in my neighborhood
rainy afternoon

scary bug hiding
on the floor
under the pile of laundry

the long night –
I sleep, while Crabtree Creek
flows on in the dark

a horse?
no thanks,
that's not for me

four a. m. –
someone from upstairs
goes outside to smoke

after the storm
lying on the ground
large magnolia blossoms

my back porch
an inviting place
for birds to sit

all is quiet
then on the radio
music begins to play

they took my back porch chair
now the birds have no place
to perch

short spring night –
the magnolias
have bloomed

old man
sees catalpa tree blossoms
for the first time

blackbird
pecking at something dead
on the rainy street

dusk's amber light
lingers
so exquisitely

so cool today
I cover my head for warmth
not for shade

a bat flits
in cool shade
under the bridge

on my back porch
bird food
a long time untouched

old man coughs and coughs
finally goes outside
to smoke some more

the homeowner
slowly enters his kitchen
afraid of more leaks

bird
lands
on a busy street

bats under the bridge –
nearby
people loitering

grandmother
you can sleep now
I'm home

that bush
looks like it's blooming
but it's really snow

the heat from my lamp –
good in winter
bad in summer

old man
grateful
to be sleeping late

a wrong turn
driving
through parking lots again

violent storm –
how do they survive,
neighborhood birds?

old pond
frogs croaking
midnight stereo

honeysuckle vines –
it's good walking east,
good walking west

the end of winter –
warm day portends
a hot summer

early spring –
so warm we need
air conditioning

walking on the trail –
I can slow down
there's no one back there

spring
too often
seems like summer

old man
awakes in the dark
with his ears ringing

after the storm
hailstones melting
in the birdbath

long ago
there was much winter rain
for my mother too

VI

headache this morning –
took two ibuprofen
then a third one

snow is falling
blanketing the neighborhood
with good cheer

sorry, spiders –
if I see you,
I must kill you

noon –
bats flying in the shade
under the bridge

gazing out my door –
like watching TV
with the sound turned off

mice
can't help but defecate
wherever they go

oh, unhappy moth –
if you let me
I'll help you get out

earwig
on my ceiling
really hard to kill

children
making snow angels
are snow angels

spiders
in my basement –
there they can stay

men
don't go through yearly cycles
like cherry trees

mice come and crap
on my kitchen counter
when the lights go off

such a nice evening
but still
it has to storm

days go by
but you learn to use
what time you can

a blue streak
glimpsed flying across the street
this evening

the moth
made the wrong decision
so I caught it

gazing at the sky —
nothing for us out there,
everything down here

dead possum
big mess
on the rainy street

away on vacation
my spiders can stop hiding
for a week

really often
cutting his grass
my next door neighbor

rainy day in May —
memories
of blue herons

cockroaches
just too fast
to catch

in this neighborhood
you can know the people
by their yards

May —
a cool day
for a change

baby mouse –
you must be sad too
since your mother died

life of the mind
always gives way
to the body

sleepy cat
suddenly alert –
mouse nearby

fifty years
day after day driving
the same streets

youth
can be beautiful
but so can old age

old man
gazing out the window
a bird flies by

my little dachshund
in the back yard
sleeping in the sun

spring mosquitoes –
they haven't bitten me yet
but some have tried

to see the sun rise,
oh my soul,
is to own the day

waking
the drone of lawn mowers
across the street

the baby spiders
from their dead mother's carcass
scurrying

old man
thankful he slept so well –
some old men don't

the smell of dinner
lingering in the air
after my nap

lying in bed
my lover mentions hearing
a distant train

full moon
over the Acropolis
when I was young

moons I've seen?
more than seven hundred
in my life so far

little flying bugs
laid eggs in my grains and beans –
disgusting larvae

spring arrives
with warmer days
and dragonflies

cockroach on the wall
fearless
now it's dead

in my yard,
leave the blackbirds alone –
they're eating bugs!

sunny Sunday
sad murder in the news
maybe god's at the beach

little red bird –
what's wrong
don't you like my crackers?

blackbird in the street
doesn't budge
as a car drives by

lizards
are such scaredy cats
and rightly so

winter's too cold
summer's too hot
I love fall and spring

Carolina moon
no different really
from any other moon

after-dinner nap
waking up stiff
and stupid

tonight
a gentle rain –
better than those storms

little squirrels
let's get one thing clear
you can't eat my house

the creatures
in my back yard
take turns being heard

I spend a lot of time
watching squirrels
and they've been watching me

visiting
my childhood home
finding it's gone

in all my days
I've missed so much
birdsong

in the spring
looking at blue sky
through a hole in my roof

blue butterfly –
writing about you
is like trying to catch you

just before dawn –
everything so quiet
even the stars

dawn freezing
fingers numb
fishing with my dad

spring flowers
never tiresome
never

autumn
start of a new school year –
the time she loved most

woodpecker
wakes up early
and wakes me up

cricket in my house
lucky, perhaps,
but annoying

I hate to go to bed
but I love to read
and I love to sleep

I miss her cooking
but most of all
I miss her face

VII

silence
between pages
books

one creek
flows into another
silence

silence
stepping from the shower
dripping

turtles
on the rocks in the creek
silence

silence
after the storm
after sunset

early autumn leaves
holding colors inside
silence

silence
around the waiting spider
a web

silence
after the hailstorm
scattered debris

red-tipped branches
spring arriving
silence

silence
then flowing over rocks
the babbling creek

down, down
the waters flowing
silence

silence
pushing lovers apart
invisibly

butterfly
perpetual fluttering
silence

moving into shadows
the firefly takes with him
starlight

rising to the moon
the firefly
brighter than a star

falling to earth
a shooting star brings with it
celestial light

gazing at shadows
memory persists
distant starlight

darkness moving
the sun casting light
and shadows

standing near a fire
feeling a chill
on your back

gazing at the fire
your back dark
like the night

some legs still twitching
after the centipede
is crushed

digging in the earth
ants
building their home

ants
love my home sometimes
more than theirs

exploring
ants find sugar
in my kitchen

I have my space
the spiders have theirs
suburban house

spiders make cobwebs
I sweep them away
we're both doing our jobs

I sweep the cobwebs
patiently
the spiders build them back

adding wings
to babies
flying angels

adding wings
to certain mobile homes
white trash aeroplanes

shooting star
reminding us that space
is not empty

meteors
more rocks for earth
'cause we don't have enough

shooting stars
marking time
until the big one comes

morning starts with song
birds in the grass
and in the trees

thunder
fireflies blinking
in the dark

after-dinner nap
in another room
a closed book

the new day arrives
birds singing
woodpeckers pecking

taking out the trash —
in the street
is that a fox running?

thunder
a fox limping
in my neighbor's yard

after-dinner nap —
streetlights and fireflies
soon in my front yard

after-dinner nap
news on the TV
going by unheard

a warm spring
long hot summer days
with hazy air

bringing down
a pinch of moonlight
a firefly

how will I find
those days so far away
so long ago?

what must it want?
red bird sitting for so long
outside my window

where has it been?
ruffled little red bird
sitting on my porch

when will he leave?
homeless friend
sleeping on my floor

back porch chair
a red bird lands on
the smell of sunshine

in Rothgeb Park
over by the creek
a blue-tailed lizard

old man grows older
as he watches
the creek flowing by

back yard chairs
seats for people
and birds

incense at dinner
bringing pollution into
the restaurant

night
firefly passes my window
blinking in the dark

summer heat
in the middle of the road
a dead possum

landing on the porch
the red bird
makes its entrance

rain ending
splashing puddles
in the driveway

silence everywhere
except
inside her head

fog hanging
in my neighborhood
a blackbird landing

standing on the curb
pinecones in the street
and in my yard

torrential rain
cleaning the air
scattering debris

dried prune faces
started out as plums
sweet and succulent

light before sunrise
same as light after sunset
yet different

photo of my dead wife
my soul
crying

VIII

December storm
my yard now covered
with leaves

from tree to tree
a blackbird flies silently
through the fog

autumn leaves blowing
in the neighborhood
children laughing

freezing new year's night
hearing the spoon clink
as my son eats hot soup

babbling Crabtree Creek
a muskrat dives
and swims on

winter twilight
the sky casts an awesome glow
upon my yard

long, quiet twilight
then the whistle
from a distant train

sunny afternoon
in the woods
snow falling from branches

winter night
bare branches silhouetted
against the sky

in the woods
the telephone rings
in my pocket

bright morning sunshine
yesterday's snow-covered street
just a memory

so cold outside
yet cherry trees bloom pink
in Cameron Village

if a black cat
is unlucky
what about a white cat?

all those spring blossoms
and she could not see
a single reason to live

morning sun shines
through bedroom blinds
upon my sleepy eyes

birds may sing, insects buzz,
but much about spring
is silent

cold winter day
homeless family in the park
cooks food on a grill

spring garden
carpet of wildflowers
and a goldfish pond

today at the lake
blackbirds instead of gulls
standing on the dock

bees
in the sun
my backyard flowers

April days
wisteria fragrance
and dangling inchworms

such a surprise
a blue heron flying
over the creek

afternoon
sunlight glints off the water
on a turtle's back

5 a. m.
I close my eyes
hoping sleep comes before dawn

distant thunder
wondering
if she hears it too

families of geese too
walk across the street –
grocery store parking lot

lonely?
no
I still have my dreams

summer sunset
worried mind
butterfly fluttering by

a leaf
dropping from the tree
a red bird

lonely
bird
lands on my back porch

summer sunset
deep in thought
mosquito at my ear

late morning wind
leaves falling
past my window

I will never know
the sound of frost
and never hope to . . .

tossing out water
working ceaselessly
ants in the yard

old pond
frog surfacing
a bubble

old pond
patiently awaiting
summer rain

spring
new green leaves
on my roof

field of white
wildflowers
butterflies

spring
already
summer

gazing through my window
missing
birdsong

flashes of lightning
beside my bed
a flashlight

ice storm
home not so homey
without lights or heat

sitting on the porch
sipping scuppernong wine
hurtling through space

a blue heron flies
over the pond
toward the setting sun

next year
when the geese return
I will be gone

catching a glimpse
of the moon
through a spider web

fog settles
over our neighborhood
for most of the day

no matter
if I'm here or gone
the geese always abide

the moon
tangled up
in a spider web

blue heron
standing in the creek
as if for a million years

out on a date –
where's the moon
when you need it?

blue heron
as if from another time
standing in the creek

speaking lightly
of the dead –
just because . . .

fireflies silent
in the dark
frogs singing

pink fallen blossoms
covering the street
at least for now

blossoms
drifting downward
butterflies

winter morning —
who has seen
the sparrow's breath?

freezing cold —
standing in the shadow
of a snowman

driving past
the graveyard
I don't slow down

not alone
in the dark
the frogs are singing

living in the city –
have I seen a cocoon
since I was a boy?

dead squirrel
in the snow
blackbird footprints

moments passing
so slow
amber twilight

watching fireflies
spending most of my time
watching darkness

put a firefly
in a jar
put out its light

blue twilight
so captivating
the green leaves

amber twilight
too fleeting
awesome glow in my yard

listening
off and on all night
for the mousetrap to snap

mushrooms in my yard
pushing up and spreading
like umbrellas

slug in my yard
crawling
on a large mushroom

cut the grass today
tonight
swatting mosquitoes

at the mailbox
finding
a tick on my hand

mosquitoes
in the dark back yard
fireflies

mid-September
autumn is coming
right?

dawn
pushing up from the soil
mushrooms

leaves
falling on my roof
autumn rain

winter air
visible breath
steamy coffee cup

immobile
in the refrigerator
summer fly

spring
fragrances returning
one blossom at a time

rattling of cans
in the recycling bin
one chagrined possum

old house
empty now
the sparrow's nest

cobweb clusters
in the grass
morning dew

afternoon
the squirrels watch me
as I drive away

summer afternoon
horses stand baking
in a field with no shade

doesn't bother me
so I don't bother it —
living room clutter

muggy morning
weeds
growing over my curb

the stars
I can't hear
their music

over the sand
chasing a beach ball
windblown

June again
her passing still hurts
even after five years

old man
glad he's finally discovered
white crape myrtles

old pond
sounds of
old frogs

early June
old pond warm enough
for drowning

old pond
my love slips into
eternal silence

old pond
my love slips in
and is gone

Notes

I started writing haiku in 2007 while working on my Master of Fine Arts degree at National University of California. Frankly I fell in love with the form. One good thing about haiku is that you can think about them anytime and anywhere. In fact, writing them sort of becomes a way of life. You can be at the mall, see somebody doing something unusual, and easily jot down a haiku. Unless you are completely wrapped up in yourself, there are numerous opportunities to write haiku. And I really believe that writing haiku could be a path to mental health. In writing them you have to focus outside yourself – observe nature, etc – and anytime you do that it is a good thing.

A person could probably read this book in one sitting and conclude that it is no big deal. But that is not the way haiku are meant to be read. They are meant to be considered carefully, and if you consider my or any haiku in more than a cursory manner, I think you are sure to find more than you expect to find.

No one is going to like all my haiku. I usually love only a handful of all the ones that I read. I do hope that you, the reader, love some of my haiku. There are certainly a lot of them here for you to choose from. If you do love some of them, then I will consider that I have succeeded with this book.

Section I. My first haiku are based on my everyday experiences: raking leaves, watching birds, etc.

Section II. In 2008 I started spending a lot of time outside in nature. When the weather was good, I usually walked for an hour per day in the parks and greenways surrounding Crabtree Creek in Raleigh, North Carolina. And the first five months of 2008 were magnificent, so I had some of my best experiences then, both personal and artistic. Gradually these nature poems merged with the other haiku I was writing, as can be seen by the variety of subject matter in the latter part of this section.

Section III. I wonder if anyone can tell the difference between the haiku in this section and the ones in the previous section. While looking at these just now I could not.

Jane Reichhold, in her book *Writing and Enjoying Haiku: a hands-on guide*, says ". . . take up each (poem in this book) and examine it carefully . . . allow the words to move across any similar memory or past idea you may have had . . . and begin here . . . to write your own versions of the poems . . . ." (7-8) Beginning with this section, that is what I did, although her instructions were a little more detailed. For section III, I read all the haiku in *Classic Haiku: a master's selection*, by Yuzuru Miura. I examined each haiku carefully, allowed the words to move across similar memories or past ideas I had, and I wrote my own versions of the poems – i.e., my own responses to their stimuli. There are about one hundred haiku in that book, and I only came up with twenty-four haiku of my own, so some of the haiku inspired me, but most did not. I had several goals: I wanted to learn something, I wanted to express myself artistically by writing my own haiku, and I hoped that you might learn something as well from my experience. One other byproduct of this process was that I also enjoyed myself a lot.

Section IV. In this section I looked at a number of haiku by Bashō, in the book *The Essential Haiku: versions of Bashō, Buson, & Issa*, edited by Poet Laureate Robert Hass. Bashō, of course, is probably the greatest haiku master of all. He wrote one of the most famous and discussed haiku ever: "old pond / a frog jumps into / the sound of water." As you read my book, you will find a good number of "old pond" haiku that I wrote. The Old Pond is a good place for nature to play itself out. It really inspired me.

There are a lot of people making money telling us how to write haiku. If you look at someone like Bashō, though, you might find that you can really throw some of that theory out the window. For example, take something like "Teeth sensitive to the sand / in salad greens / I'm getting old." (47) To me that seems to violate much of what people tell us about writing haiku, except that it is three lines, and basically 5-7-5 syllables (7-4-4, actually, but who's counting?) It does not seem to be an image, in the usual sense of that term, and most of the effectiveness of haiku depends on the image, visual, auditory, etc. This haiku really is just a statement of what is on an old man's mind, stated succinctly and within certain formal constraints. There's nothing wrong with that. In fact, I think it is great. It means we are free from much of the advice given in haiku books, free to express ourselves spontaneously. Of course Bashō's technique in this haiku is subtle, and that is why he is a master. I guess a further point is, if you want to learn how to write haiku, look at the old masters, see what they did, and do something similar. That is what Jane Reichhold seems to think we should do, and it is what I have tried to do with this book. (While I'm thinking about it, let me just say that a lot of it has to do with simplicity. A lot of people, when they begin to write haiku, write complex poems in 5-7-5 format. The more you learn, however, the more you understand the value of simplicity.)

One of my haiku from this section (rainy evening / home alone with tears / chopping onions) was published in *The Chapel Hill News*, April 23, 2008.

Section V. I learned a lot from Buson. Often, for him, there are three elements to his haiku, and one element goes on each line. For example, 1) in the summer rain 2) the path 3) has disappeared. Many poets might have tried to complicate this, but Buson keeps it very simple. He could have combined 2 and 3, and added another element, but then he would have had four. I didn't write so many haiku under Buson's influence, but I really think I learned a lot from him.

Section VI. Issa is the next master from the Hass book that I deal with. I suppose there are two main things about Issa: his simplicity and his humor, both of which I greatly admire. I don't really have a lot to say about him except that he is very entertaining and I like him a lot.

Section VII. This section, as I mentioned above, was influenced by Jane Reichhold's book *Writing and Enjoying Haiku*. Jane is a longtime and highly respected member of the haiku community. Her book may be the best instructional book around, although I have not read them all. If you do read them all you find that you get all these people telling you how to write haiku, sometimes with conflicting advice, and you should really just be living your life and writing haiku. Reading haiku that others have written is also helpful.

There are not a lot of haiku in Reichhold's book. Often she gives you exercises to do, or a bit of theory with examples. (Be sure to look at the 'silence' haiku, pages 8-10, of her book, and compare them with mine.) Toward the middle of her book (55-70) she elaborates twenty-four different ways of writing haiku, with examples. This is very helpful. You can tell that she has really made an in-depth study of this subject.

Section VIII. The final book that I looked at was *Haiku Moment: an anthology of contemporary North American haiku,* edited by Bruce

Ross. There are over 800 haiku in his book, and I only got fewer than a hundred haiku of my own out of the exercise. Reviewers of this book have said it is "a landmark work," "an impressive collection of haiku," and that "Ross has done a remarkably thorough job." I agree. I recommend that you read this and all the books mentioned here.